10ℇ

CONSIDER THE LEMMING

CONSIDER
THE LEMMING

JEANNE STEIG

Pictures by **WILLIAM STEIG**

Michael di Capua Books

Farrar, Straus and Giroux

New York

To my children,
Bill, Terry, and Maggie

THE ELEPHANT

It's easy to identify
The elephant—I'll tell you why.
The elephant has tiny eyes,
Considering his mammoth size;
His tail is like a piece of string;
And there's another funny thing:
The ludicrously baggy pants
Peculiar to elephants.

THE HARE

Befriending the hare is not easy.
He is skittish and tends to get queasy.
But persist! You will find
He's enchantingly kind
And never does anything sleazy.

Yes, it's hard to make friends with the hare,
For he tends to get twitchy and stare.
But the hare is true blue.
When accustomed to you,
He'll prove witty, discreet, debonair.

THE PIG

The pig is held in ill repute;
He's thought to be a coarse-grained brute.
A slurper-up of slops, the swine,
He's never asked indoors to dine.
But if the loathsome pig were fed
On marzipan and fine white bread,
And if he were allowed to shower
And dust himself with scented flour,
And spend a week in Cannes or Florence,
Would we still hold him in abhorrence?
Or would we find ourselves recanting,
And cry: "Oh, Pig, thou art enchanting!"

THE GIRAFFE

The giraffe, said the weary Creator,
Is not such a klutz as the gator.
But his legs, when he trots,
Might get tied up in knots.
Perhaps I will shorten them later.

THE BEAVER

A builder of dams is the beaver.
He toils at his task in a fever.
He can gnaw through a tree
While you pour the Chablis.
He's a consummate overachiever.

FISH

Of all the million kinds of fish,
There is not one will grant a wish
The way, in fairy tales, they used to.
Beg all you like, they just refuse to.

They don't hand out enchanted castles,
Nor golden swords with fancy tassels.
No prophecies! No sage advice!
Fish of today belong on ice.

THE CAT

No need to introduce the cat;
You've got one lying on your mat.
Ailurophobes, of course, do not.
They'd rather see cats hanged or shot.

The cat's detractors can't abide
The creature's overweening pride.
Admirers of the feline praise
His occult, incandescent gaze.

Both sides have merit—and the view
Endorsed by mice is also true.

THE RHINOCEROS

The skin of the rhino is thick,
Yet he trembles at insects that prick.
So he wallows in mud
When the river's at flood—
A sloppy but sensible trick.

THE DOG

Which pet is most beloved by man?
The cat? The horse? The ortolan?
The chimpanzee? The winsome hog?
Not on your life! It is the dog.

At certain tasks the dog excels,
Like pulling babies out of wells
And finding travelers in the snow
And fetching things that people throw.

What energy the dog expends
In welcoming your foes and friends!
A noble beast when at his best!
At other times, alas, a pest.

THE MOCKINGBIRD

Can any soul remain unstirred
When listening to the mockingbird?
Ofttimes at 3 a.m. he'll start
To pour his imitative heart
Into the wakeful, ravished ear
And sing for hours with monstrous cheer
Cacophonies that he collects,
And comic-opera side effects.
And catcalls, whistles, razzmatazz—
Oh, what a repertoire he has!
He is a one-bird cabaret.
Hip hip, Blithe Spirit! Hip hooray!

THE LEMMING

Consider the lemming:
No hawing or hemming
No dilly or dally
No shilly or shally
The whole lemming nation
In one wild migration
Is off to the sea.

He can't swim, the lemming,
And yet there's no stemming
His rush to the water.
A lem to the slaughter!
Don't ask him "Who sent ya?"
It must be dementia—
Unless it's ennui.

THE MOLE

One rarely gets to meet the mole,
He's such a misanthropic soul.
He tunnels blindly in the earth
And nothing knows of warmth or mirth.
A few close friends? No. Please excuse him—
Not even other moles amuse him.

THE PARROT

The parrot, untutored, can't speak,
Not English, Swahili, or Greek.
But when taught, he'll discourse
With rhetorical force,
Though his syntax remains a bit weak.

THE PENGUIN

The penguin, who looks so romantic,
So dapper in white tie and tails,
Behaves in a manner most antic.
I refer to both females and males.

The penguin (You'll think I am jesting.
Would it sound more convincing in prose?)
Just cannot be bothered with nesting,
So he carries her eggs on his toes.

THE SNAIL

Concerning the snail and his cousin, the slug,
Not much may be said in their favor.
In the matter of looks, one is apt to cry "Ugh!"
Though the snail has a delicate flavor.
Both gastropods keep a tentacular eye
On the lookout for raven or crow
As they slither through life on one foot, which is why
They are, both of them, damnably slow.

THE STORK

They say it is the stork who brings
New babies, tucked in little slings.
Good heavens, what a shameless lie!
The stork has other fish to fry.
Each spring he and his wife enjoy
Remodeling their nest. Oh, boy!
Those nests get big and full of eggs,
Which turn to chicks on skinny legs.
They clack their beaks and act so rude,
With all their clamoring for food,
The poor old stork gets quite unstrung
Just trying to placate his young.
His wings are weak, his vision's blurred.
Deliver babies? How absurd.

THE OPOSSUM

The opossum, as everyone knows,
Is prehensile of tail and of toes.
It carries its young in a pocket
And plays dead if you happen to shock it.
The opossum is ugly and vicious.
Fricasseed, it is highly nutritious.

THE SLOTH

There's nothing saucy
About the sloth. He

Is always sleepy.
Isn't that creepy?

THE CROCODILE

When seeking out the crocodile,
Head for the Ganges or the Nile.
Wait till a mossy log drifts by
And fixes you with bulbous eye.
Well, there's your croc. He's sure to grin.
Don't let yourself be taken in.
His teeth are sharp, his breath is fetid.
His appetite is quickly whetted!

THE CAMEL*

The camel's not a pretty sight
Unless you've wandered through the night
O'er trackless sands and lost a shoe—
Then maybe he'll look good to you.

Don't try to start a conversation.
Save yourself the aggravation.
Although his back's commodious,
His disposition's odious.

*One hump, you're on a dromedary;
 Two, a camel. Both are hairy.

THE WEASEL

The weasel is clever, the weasel is spunky,
The weasel when peeved smells decidedly funky.
He's long in the torso and short in the legs.
He's a merciless hunter—they say he sucks eggs.

In summer the weasel, like ferret and stoat,
Goes out in a nondescript frumpy brown coat.
But if, as may happen, his winter vacation
Is spent in a more or less frigid location,

An astounding transmogrification occurs:
The weasel puts on the most luscious of furs.
He turns into an ermine! How does he achieve it?
A fact is a fact, you can take it or leave it.

BIG SNAKES

It doesn't pay to get too fonda
Your python or your anaconda.

THE MANTICORE

A mythic beast, the manticore—
Dragon behind and man before,
With lion sandwiched in between 'em.
No living soul has ever seen him,
Nor any combination of
The creatures in the list above.

THE BULL

We talk about the bull a lot.
We mention how much strength he's got,
How prone to fits of rage when taunted,
How, in a china shop, unwanted.
We take him by the horns in daring
And name him when we fall to swearing.
Sometimes we shoot the bull. Poor Taurus!
He must—how could he not—abhor us.

MAN

Adam and Eve, who first began
The human race, the race of man,
Walked upright, and had brains and thumbs.
(We use those still, for doing sums.)
They named the beasts, invented clothes,
Left Eden, when the need arose.
The need arose in apple season.
It's called the Fall, for just that reason.

FIN